MW01107057

INTELLECTUAL PROPERTY PROTECTION

SECOND EDITION

—A Guide for Engineers—

David S. Goldstein
Virginia Shaw Medlen, J.D.

PROFESSIONAL PUBLICATIONS, INC.
Belmont, CA 94002

In the ENGINEERING REFERENCE MANUAL SERIES

Engineer-In-Training Reference Manual
  Engineering Fundamentals Quick Reference Cards
  Engineer-In-Training Sample Examinations
  Mini-Exams for the E-I-T Exam
  1001 Solved Engineering Fundamentals Problems
  E-I-T Review: A Study Guide
Civil Engineering Reference Manual
  Civil Engineering Quick Reference Cards
  Civil Engineering Sample Examination
  Civil Engineering Review Course on Cassettes
  Seismic Design of Building Structures
  Seismic Design Fast
  Timber Design for the Civil P.E. Examination
  Fundamentals of Reinforced Masonry Design
  246 Solved Structural Engineering Problems
Mechanical Engineering Reference Manual
  Mechanical Engineering Quick Reference Cards
  Mechanical Engineering Sample Examination
  101 Solved Mechanical Engineering Problems
  Mechanical Engineering Review Course on Cassettes
  Consolidated Gas Dynamics Tables
Electrical Engineering Reference Manual
  Electrical Engineering Quick Reference Cards
  Electrical Engineering Sample Examination
Chemical Engineering Reference Manual
  Chemical Engineering Quick Reference Cards
  Chemical Engineering Practice Exam Set
Land Surveyor Reference Manual
Petroleum Engineering Practice Problem Manual
Expanded Interest Tables
Engineering Law, Design Liability, and Professional Ethics
Engineering Unit Conversions

In the ENGINEERING CAREER ADVANCEMENT SERIES

How to Become a Professional Engineer
The Expert Witness Handbook—A Guide for Engineers
Getting Started as a Consulting Engineer
Intellectual Property Protection—A Guide for Engineers
E-I-T/P.E. Course Coordinator's Handbook
Becoming a Professional Engineer

INTELLECTUAL PROPERTY PROTECTION—A Guide for Engineers
Second Edition

Printed in the United States of America

ISBN: 0-912045-46-9

Professional Publications, Inc.
1250 Fifth Avenue, Belmont, CA 94002
(415) 593-9119

Current printing of this edition (last number): 6 5 4 3 2 1

PREFACE
to the Second Edition

This book is meant to be a guide to engineers who want to protect their intellectual property. While it is designed to provide accurate and authoritative information, it is not a substitute for legal advice or expert assistance. This is because the law, like life, is constantly evolving. Unless you keep up with the changes (and few of the engineers with whom I am acquainted have the time for such a task), you will need to consult with a professional who does.

This new edition has been rewritten and updated in response to the changes that have occurred since the first edition was published. Government fees have increased significantly, almost across the board, and will continue to go up. You should call the responsible government agency, or ask your intellectual property attorney, before relying upon any of the fees listed in the appendices. Substantive changes have occurred in the federal laws affecting trademarks and copyrights. The term of new federal trademark registrations has decreased, and the "Intent-To-Use" trademark application procedure has been adopted, which for the first time permits the "reservation" of trademarks. The Berne convention for the protection of copyrights has been adopted by the United States, changing some of the requirements for protecting copyrighted works. The rights of intellectual property owners have also been modified by the way in which courts have interpreted the intellectual property statutes.

The right of employers to the intellectual property created by their employees, or by independent contractors hired by them for that purpose, continues to be a minefield for the unwary, as does the protection of trade secrets. As two engineers formerly employed by a large Texas firm recently found out after years of litigation and appeals following a criminal conviction, a departing employee should always ask before taking anything from his or her employer that might be a trade secret or other kind of intellectual property.

Intellectual property litigation continues to be a relatively expensive affair. This, more than any other reason, is why the services of a competent intellectual property attorney should be sought as soon as possible if you are at all uncertain of your rights to intellectual property or unsure of how best to protect your intellectual property. In the law, as in medicine, prevention is always cheaper than a cure.

Virginia Shaw Medlen, J.D.
San Francisco, CA
March 1992

PROFESSIONAL PUBLICATIONS, INC. ● Belmont, CA

PREFACE
to the First Edition

This book is meant to be a guide for engineers who want to protect their intellectual property. It is not meant to be legal advice, or to be a substitute for professional legal counsel.

I have chosen to use only masculine pronouns throughout the text of this book. While I am aware that women become engineers and attorneys, and are as concerned about protecting intellectual property as are their male counterparts, I feel using he/she or any other awkward form of pronoun would make the book too difficult to read. From the beginning, simplicity has been paramount in this venture. I beg the pardon of anyone offended.

David S. Goldstein
Belmont, CA
January 1986

PROFESSIONAL PUBLICATIONS, INC. ● Belmont, CA

TABLE OF CONTENTS

Patents

Trade Secrets

PROFESSIONAL PUBLICATIONS, INC. ● Belmont, CA

INTRODUCTION

An engineer's job requires creativity. So, it is likely that during your career as an engineer, you will invent or write something. You also might design a symbol or trademark. These works are examples of *intellectual property*. The types of intellectual property you might want to protect include the following:

- literary works
- computer software
- audiotapes
- films and records
- trademarks and trade names
- trade secrets
- semiconductor chips, including read-only memory chips (ROMs), and the mask works used to produce them
- inventions

USING THE LAW AND LAWYERS
Creating intellectual property requires time and effort. It is only fair that you benefit from your effort. Ownership of intellectual property gives you certain rights. However, it is up to you to protect your work from unauthorized use. This book will tell you how.

Of course, the safest way to protect something is to lock it up and never use it or show it to anyone. That will rarely be to your advantage, however. The next safest plan is to protect your intellectual property by carefully applying the law.

Constitutional basis. Laws protecting intellectual property derive their authority from Article I, Section 8 of the U.S. Constitution.

The Congress shall have power . . . to promote the progress of science and useful arts, by securing for limited times to authors and inventors the exclusive right to their respective writings and discoveries.

Do you need a lawyer? You might be surprised how easy Congress has made it in some cases to protect your own work. It might be simply a matter of filing the proper forms and paying a recording or application fee. In some cases, however, it might be necessary to hire an attorney who specializes in intellectual property protection.

Some works, such as books, can be protected without the assistance of a lawyer. Other types of intellectual property require expert attention almost from the beginning. The need for a lawyer early in the process is especially important if you want to protect an invention. Having a lawyer conduct a patent search at an early stage might save you from reinventing something already patented.

If you have intellectual property rights that you feel are being infringed, you probably will need a lawyer to handle your case. You cannot easily fight an infringement case without an attorney.

Otherwise, the decision to seek legal counsel is up to you. Be sure to take into consideration the complexity of the application process for your kind of intellectual property. For instance, assuring copyright protection for an article you have written for a trade journal will require simply affixing the appropriate copyright notice to the work. Registering the copyright with the federal government will require only filling out a form and paying a small fee. Patenting an invention will be more difficult.

COPYRIGHTS

Literary works constitute one of the best-known forms of intellectual property, and perhaps are the simplest to protect. These include published and unpublished fiction and nonfiction such as textbooks, reference works, directories, catalogs, advertising copy, compilations of information, drawings and other designs, photographs, mask works, and computer programs. These and other nondramatic works can be protected simply by affixing the appropriate copyright notice to the work. You can register the copyright with the federal government. (The specific application forms for protecting periodicals and serials differ slightly. The forms for protecting dramatic works also differ, but are not discussed here.)

WHO CAN CLAIM THE COPYRIGHT

The *copyright* is used to protect virtually anything you might write. Generally speaking, you can claim a copyright if you are the author of a work, and you can claim a copyright in that part of a collaborative effort that you wrote. If the collaborative work cannot be split into separately authored sections, then all authors can claim a copyright in the whole work.

Works-made-for-hire. According to the law, the *author* is not always the person who wrote a given work. In some situations, the author can be the employer of the person who created the work, or the person who commissioned the work from an independent contractor. For example, an employee who writes something for his employer is not the author of the writing: the employer is. A *work-made-for-hire* is defined by the law as:

- a work prepared by an employee within the scope of employment
- a work specially ordered or commissioned, if the parties expressly agree in a written agreement made in advance of the creation of the work that the work shall be considered a work-made-for-hire, and if the work is

- a contribution to a collective work
- a part of a motion picture or other audiovisual work
- a translation
- a supplementary work
- a compilation
- an instructional text
- a test
- answer material for a test
- an atlas

Other works cannot be works-made-for-hire. Agreements made after the creation of the work can affect ownership, but cannot affect authorship of the work.

REGISTERING YOUR COPYRIGHT
A copyright arises upon the creation of the work. If, however, you wish to enforce your copyright by seeking injunctive relief or damages against someone who is using your work without your permission, you must have registered the copyright.

You can register your copyright by filing the proper form with the U.S. Copyright Office, located in the Library of Congress in Washington, D.C. If your work has been published, you need to submit two copies of it (each bearing the appropriate copyright notice) with the application. If it has not been published, only one is needed. You also must include a fee.[1]

Publication. To the Copyright Office, *publication* means the distribution of copies of a work on a nonconfidential basis to anyone, such as to the public by sale, rental, lease, or lending. It does not require that the work be professionally printed and bound.

Fixed and tangible form. To be considered published, your work must also meet the *fixed and tangible form* requirement. This stipulates that the work must be in permanent form, such as in print or on a recording. You cannot consider an impromptu speech to be published unless you write it down, and you cannot consider a song or musical piece to be published unless you produce it as sheet music or as a recording. Therefore, you cannot register copyrights in these intangible forms of intellectual property.

---

[1]A fee schedule appears in Appendix B.

Registering your copyright with the Copyright Office is straightforward. You can get the proper forms, which are free, by requesting the type and quantity of forms you need from the Copyright Office's Information and Publication Section.[2] You also can call the Copyright Office to request forms.

Forms. The Copyright Office publishes different forms for different categories of copyrightable material.

- Form TX, for nondramatic literary works
- Form VA, for works of visual art, such as illustrations or photographs
- Form GR/CP, to be used with Form TX or VA, for a group of works you are contributing to periodicals

You must use form RE to renew a copyright granted while the 1909 Copyright Act was in effect (prior to January 1, 1978). You need form CA to correct or supplement a previously filed form.

Expedited registration. If one of your previously unregistered works needs to be registered quickly (e.g., if litigation or a contract are pending), you can expedite the registration. This requires a letter from an attorney certifying that you require and are eligible for an expedited registration. If qualified, your work will be registered within five working days. This action requires an additional fee.

CORRECTING ERRORS   Under the 1909 copyright law, errors in the copyright process often resulted in loss of copyright protection. Failure to deposit a copy of a work meant loss of protection, as did using an improper copyright notice.

Under the 1976 copyright (works created between January 1, 1978 and March 1, 1989) law, however, the penalties for mistakes are less severe. You need only to file Form CA with the Copyright Office, with the proper fee, to correct or amplify the original registration. Time is of the essence, however. Leaving an incomplete, incorrect, or improper copyright notice or registration for too long might diminish your protection. You are excused for making omissions on a relatively small number of copies, but, because this standard is vague, your best bet is to correct the error as best and as quickly as you can. Also, some copyright notice defects which were made prior to

---

[2]Important addresses and phone numbers are listed in Appendix A.

March 1, 1989 must be corrected within five years, or else the work might permanently forfeit protection.

TERM OF PROTECTION

The new copyright law changed the term of the protection given by copyrights. The term thus depends on whether the work was copyrighted while the old law was in effect, or after.

Under the 1976 and 1989 Copyright Acts. Works that are created on or after January 1, 1978 are protected automatically and immediately upon creation.[3] If created in portions at different times, each portion of a work is protected immediately upon its completion.

Generally, copyright protection lasts for the author's life plus 50 years. If more than one person collaborated on a work, the term extends 50 years beyond the last surviving author's death.

Works-made-for-hire and works whose authors do not identify themselves to the Copyright Office are protected for 75 years from the date of publication, or 100 years from the date of creation, whichever occurs first.

Under the old law. The term of protection differs for works copyrighted before January 1, 1978. Under the 1909 law, copyright protection became effective on the date the work was published, or, if the work was unpublished, on the date of registration.[4] Protection lasts 28 years from the date it was secured. The copyright is renewable in the last (28th) year of its first term. The new law extends the renewal term of copyrights secured before 1978 to 47 years, making the total protection term 75 years.

RENEWALS

To process extended renewals for works copyrighted before 1978, the Copyright Office requires Form RE. The Copyright Office does not need another copy of the work. Failure to file for renewal during the year in which a pre-1978 copyright expires permanently forfeits protection beyond the year of expiration. For example, a work copyrighted in 1970 would be eligible for renewal in 1998. Because the new

---

[3]The Copyright Act of 1976 became effective January 1, 1978.

[4]The Copyright Act of 1976 superseded the Copyright Act of 1909.

copyright law extends the renewal term to 47 years instead of 28, a renewed copyright would last until 2045. If the copyright owner fails to file for renewal in 1998, he will lose protection forever after that year.

Works that were created before 1978, but were not registered, can be simultaneously registered and renewed by submitting the required documents and fees for both. The copyright term will be the author's life plus 50 years.

Who can renew a copyright. Copyright renewals can be claimed by the author if he is living, or, if the author is deceased, by the author's spouse or children. If a deceased author has no surviving spouse or child, and the author left a will, the executor of the author's estate can renew a copyright. If the author left no will, or if the estate already has been distributed, the appropriate next of kin can renew the copyright.

If a work's copyright owner is not the person who wrote the work, the copyright owner can renew the copyright only under certain conditions. He can renew the copyright in a posthumous work, a periodical, a cyclopedic or other composite work, a work copyrighted by a corporation otherwise than as an assignee or licensee of the individual author, or a work copyrighted by an employer for whom the work was made-for-hire.

WHAT CAN BE COPYRIGHTED

There is a critical distinction concerning what you can and cannot copyright. You cannot copyright ideas, concepts, or facts. You can copyright only the original expression of these ideas, concepts, or facts. For example, you cannot copyright the fact that the Dodgers beat the Yankees in 10 innings, but you can copyright a written report describing the game, provided the prose is your own. Similarly, you cannot copyright an idea for a technical journal article you'd like to write, but you can copyright the article once you've written it.

Titles cannot be copyrighted. This does not mean that anyone may freely use the titles of your works. If someone uses your title in order to mislead people into thinking his work is yours, you might have the basis for a lawsuit on the grounds that he is "palming off" his work for yours. But if he does not intend to fool people—say, he simply likes the title and intends to reach a different audience—then you might have no recourse.

Blank forms and other items. You also cannot copyright blank forms, names, short phrases, slogans, lettering, coloring, lists of contents, processes or devices, or works that consist solely of common property, containing no original authorship (e.g., standard calendars, charts, or schedules). However, you can copyright the original, literary text on otherwise uncopyrightable items.

Items in the public domain. You also cannot copyright works in the *public domain*. These are works that already have been distributed and, for one reason or another, are not protected by a copyright. For instance, a work whose copyright term has expired and has not been renewed enters the public domain, and is forever available for any use. Once a work enters the public domain, it stays there.

Works that were never copyrighted and are no longer eligible to obtain a copyright also enter the public domain. An anthology or other collective work consisting of an assembly of works in the public domain, however, might be eligible for copyright protection.

If you obtained your copyright before January 1, 1978, you must renew your copyright during the one-year period of renewal eligibility to prevent your work from entering the public domain.

Government publications. You may freely extract from government publications when you write. The Copyright Office states, however, that if you publish a work that contains significant material from government publications, your copyright notice should indicate which parts of the work are yours. Your copyright does not cover the portions extracted from government publications.

Misconceptions. Several misconceptions about copyrights exist. One is that a work must be entirely unique to be copyrighted. In fact, you can copyright a work that is similar to another if you did not copy the other work. The courts will decide if your work is too similar to another to be original, if the other author sues you for infringement.

Another misconception is that to protect your work you must register it with the federal government. Actually, you may consider your original work copyrighted the instant you write it. For maximum legal protection, however, you will need to register your copyright.

MISCELLANEOUS WORKS

There are several other types of works that engineers might need to copyright. Each type is handled differently.

Drawings. Drawings and text must be copyrighted separately. You must submit Form VA (used for published or unpublished works of the visual arts) to register your drawings. You need to send Form TX (for published or unpublished nondramatic literary works) to register your text.

Audiovisual works. Registering audiovisual works is similar to registering literary works. For pictorial, graphic, and sculptural works, use Form VA. For motion pictures and other audiovisual works, use Form PA.

New versions of existing works. A copyright protecting a new version of a previously copyrighted work covers only the new material. The author is the person who created the new material. If the author of the new material is different from the original version's author, only the new author may renew a copyright in that portion of the work.

UNPUBLISHED WORKS

You do not need to publish a work to copyright it. Even an unpublished work is considered copyrighted upon its creation. In fact, you do not even need to publish a work to register it with the Copyright Office. All forms used to register published works also can be used for unpublished ones.

This has not always been the case. Under the 1909 act, a work had to be published to be registered, and the work had to be registered to enable the copyright owner to sue in a federal court for infringement. States had varying degrees of protection for unpublished works, but publication was a prerequisite for federal protection under the 1909 act. The federal act automatically became effective when a work was first published.

The new copyright law extends protection to unpublished works. You might find advantages to registering your unpublished works. The most obvious, of course, is that you have the maximum federal protection. However, registering your work—whether published or unpublished—with the Copyright Office means anyone can gain access to your work and read it. The Privacy Act Advisory Statement found on copyright registration forms says anything you write on that form will be used to establish and maintain a public record.

The work you submit with the form is also considered public. Therefore, do not register any work that you do not want the public to read.

If your previously registered, unpublished work gets published, you do not need to reregister the work, but you may do so if you wish. The Copyright Office will need two copies of the published version, should you desire to reregister it.

COPYRIGHT NOTICE
For works created prior to March 1, 1989, the copyright notice requirement is simple but crucial. It indicates to others that your work is copyrighted and that they cannot copy it without your permission. There are three acceptable forms of copyright notice: the word "Copyright," the symbol ©, and the abbreviation "Copyr." All three forms require the year and the name of the copyright owner. For example, the following three copyright notices result in the same protection in the U.S.

> Copyright 1985 John Doe
> © 1985 John Doe
> Copyr. 1985 John Doe

International notice. While any one of these forms legally protects you in the U.S., only the © form, followed by the sentence, "All rights reserved," offers the maximum international protection.[5] Such a notice would look like this:

> © 1985 John Doe. All rights reserved.

Anonymous, pseudonymous, and collaborative registration. If you wish to remain anonymous, you can use a copyright notice like this:

> © 1985 Anonymous

It is legal to withhold your name even from the Copyright Office, but to do so limits the copyright term to 75 years from the date of publication. If you

---

[5]The phrase, "All rights reserved," protects you in the following countries, which are parties to the Buenos Aires Convention (BAC) of 1910: Argentina, Bolivia, Brazil, Chile, Colombia, Costa Rica, Dominican Republic, Ecuador, Guatemala, Haiti, Honduras, Mexico, Nicaragua, Panama, Paraguay, Peru, and Uruguay.

remain anonymous on the work itself but reveal your name to the Copyright Office, you are entitled to the usual term—your life plus 50 years.

You also can register your copyright under a pseudonym. The pseudonym would be the name on the copyright notice. The same copyright term limitation applies to a pseudonymous author as to an anonymous one.

For a collaborative work (one that you write with one or more other people), the notice should contain all authors' names. For a collective work (a collection of separate works by different authors), separate notices should be listed together, each containing one author's name, the year he published his part of the work, and the © symbol.

Phonorecords of Sound Recordings. The form of copyright notice on phonorecords is similar and consists of three elements:

- ℗
- Year of first publication
- Name of the copyright owner

For works created under the new copyright act (on or after March 1, 1989), copyright notice is not required. However, including a notice in the form described above is still desirable since it prevents an infringer from avoiding actual or statutory damages by claiming innocent infringement.

Registering unpublished works. The copyright notice is unnecessary for unpublished works, but it is a good idea to affix a notice (such as the following) to all copies that leave your hands. This will help avoid unintentional, unauthorized publication.

Unpublished Work © 1985 John Doe

Works distributed in pieces. If you wish to protect works that you distribute in pieces, register each piece separately and place a copyright notice on each piece as you distribute it. This applies in cases such as class notes distributed weekly, portions of design plans given to a client over a period of time, and other similarly distributed works.

Items of negligible value. Registering copyrights involves time, effort, and money. In most cases, registration does not require great amounts of any of these, but registering works of little or no value might not be worthwhile.

YOUR RIGHTS

What does a copyright do for you? It gives you the exclusive right to the following:

- To reproduce the copyrighted work
- To prepare derivative works based upon the copyrighted work
- To sell, rent, lease, or lend copies to the public
- To publicly display the copyrighted work

Advantages to registering. Although the 1976 copyright law affords you significant protection without requiring you to register with the Copyright Office, there are several advantages to registering. It publicly establishes your copyright and enables you to sue infringers. Registration also establishes the validity of your copyright if the work is published without a copyright notice, provided the work is registered within five years of publication. Furthermore, registration enables you to collect statutory damages and attorney's fees in addition to actual damages and profits in successful infringement suits, if the work is registered within three months of publication or prior to the infringement.

Registration is a prerequisite to an infringement suit unless the infringed work is a Berne Convention work whose country of origin is not the U.S.; the application, fee, and deposit were delivered to the Copyright Office in proper form and registration was refused; or the infringed work consists of sounds, images, or both, the first fixation of which was made simultaneously with its transmission.

Transferring a copyright. A copyright signifies ownership. Therefore, you may sell, license, trade, or transfer by any other means, the rights to your work. If the copyright is owned jointly, a co-owner may transfer only the portion of the copyright that he owns.

When registration becomes valid. Copyright registration becomes valid on the date the Copyright Office receives everything it needs in acceptable form. The Copyright Office will not send a confirmation that it received your documents, but it will return a self-addressed, postage-paid postcard that indicates the date your application was received, if you enclose the card with your application. It might take three or more months to receive a registration certificate or a rejection and explanation.

WHERE YOU ARE PROTECTED Copyright protection in the U.S. covers all of your unpublished works, regardless of your nationality and in what country you live. A published work is protected in the U.S. if one or more of the authors is a U.S. citizen or resident on the work's first publication date, or is a citizen or resident of a foreign country that has signed a copyright treaty with the U.S. A work also is protected if it is first published in the U.S. or in a foreign country that is a member of the Universal Copyright Convention (UCC) or the Berne Convention on the first publication date.[6]

Foreign protection. Protecting a work in other countries requires a different strategy. Unfortunately, some countries like China, Saudi Arabia, and Iran offer little or no protection for U.S. works. No international copyright exists. However, many countries, including the U.S., belong to the UCC and the Berne Convention, and all member countries agree to honor copyrights granted by all other member countries, as long as each copyrighted work bears the © symbol, the name of the copyright owner, and the year of the work's first publication. In addition, the phrase "All rights reserved," placed below the copyright notice, is required to protect your work in Buenos Aires Convention (BAC) countries.

Also, the U.S. maintains bilateral copyright agreements with some countries. You can obtain a current list from the Copyright Office's Information and Publications Section.

If you are interested in protecting your work in a particular country, you should investigate that country's procedures for copyrighting. It would be best to do this before your work is published anywhere, because protection often depends on the circumstances surrounding initial publication.

---

[6]UCC members are Algeria, Andorra, Argentina, Australia, Austria, Bahamas, Bangladesh, Barbados, Belgium, Belize, Brazil, Bulgaria, Cameroon, Canada, Chile, Colombia, Costa Rica, Cuba, Czechoslovakia, Denmark, Dominican Republic, Ecuador, El Salvador, Fiji, Finland, France, Germany, Ghana, Greece, Guatemala, Guinea, Haiti, Hungary, Iceland, India, Ireland, Israel, Italy, Japan, Kampuchea, Kenya, Laos, Lebanon, Liberia, Liechtenstein, Luxembourg, Malawi, Malta, Mauritius, Mexico, Monaco, Morocco, Netherlands, New Zealand, Nicaragua, Nigeria, Norway, Pakistan, Panama, Paraguay, Peru, Poland, Portugal, Senegal, Spain, Sri Lanka, Sweden, Switzerland, Tunisia, U.K., U.S., U.S.S.R., Vatican City, Venezuela, Yugoslavia, and Zambia.

INFRINGEMENT   A copyright gives you exclusive rights to reproduce your work in virtually any format. If someone violates your right, you have cause to sue for infringement. To sue someone you believe is an infringer of your copyright, you will need to register your work and probably will need to hire a lawyer.

Injunctions and restraining orders. As a first step, you can get the court to issue you a temporary injunction or restraining order, but only if your copyright is federally registered. A simple hearing in which you exhibit the copyright registration certificate itself is often all it takes to have the court issue an injunction against further infringement. This injunction will protect you while you are waiting for the case to go to court.

Writ of attachment. If you feel that the defendant is likely to move his assets out of the country to prevent losing them to you in court, you can ask a judge to issue a *writ of attachment*. This order prevents the defendant from moving his funds until a subsequent trial concludes.

In court. In addition to proving that the defendant copied your work, you also need to prove that you own the copyright. This part is relatively simple, because you must have registered the work in the Copyright Office in order to have initiated the lawsuit. The courts consider registration with the Copyright Office to be sufficient evidence that you own the copyright.

The ease with which you can prove the defendant copied your work depends largely on whether he used your words verbatim or paraphrased your work. The former, of course, is much easier to show. If the latter is the case, you must prove that the defendant had access to your work (which might be tricky, if your work is unpublished) and you must convince the jury that the two works are similar enough that the defendant must have copied your work. The court will evaluate similarity of structure and of expression in determining whether a verdict is warranted in your favor.

Winning the case. If you win the case, the court will issue a judgment against the infringer, preventing him from producing any more copies of the infringing work. The court also might award you actual damages (in an amount that the court believes you have lost because of the infringement) or the profits the infringer made by copying your work.

You have another option if your lawsuit is successful. Instead of accepting actual damages, you can request statutory damages, which allows the judge to decide how much to award you. Ordinarily, statutory damages range from $500 to $20,000, although for willful infringement, the maximum can range up to $100,000. The minimum award for innocent infringement is $200. The amount usually depends on the extent of infringement and on whether or not the infringement was intentional. You might also collect attorney's fees in addition to statutory damages. You cannot collect statutory damages or attorney's fees unless you registered your copyright before the infringement began.

Fair use. Some uses of a copyrighted work are allowable, however. These fall under the fair use section of the copyright law. This section says that using copyrighted material for criticism, comment, news reporting, teaching (including multiple copies for classroom use), scholarship, or research, does not constitute infringement. The section specifies the criteria by which to judge fair use:

- Was the material used for commercial purposes, or for nonprofit educational purposes?
- What is the nature of the copyrighted work?
- What proportion of the copyrighted work was used?
- How has using the copyrighted material affected its potential market value?

Photocopying. Photocopying all or part of a copyrighted work, unless it is done for one of the purposes considered fair use, is an infringement of copyright. This is one of the most common modes of copyright infringement.

Book piracy. Unlike most cases of infringement, which involve illegally copying portions of a protected work, book piracy is the reproduction of entire texts. Book piracy takes two primary forms: printed book piracy and unauthorized photocopying. The former is the unauthorized publishing of a book whose copyright belongs to someone else. The latter is the wholesale photocopying of entire works. Both practices are widespread, especially in some Asian and Latin American countries.

American publishers have been trying to curb book piracy, particularly by negotiating with the governments of the countries most often cited as piracy nations. The publishers have been largely unsuccessful. The main problem is that international law does not consider intellectual property appropriation to be theft.

What can you do if you suspect your work is being pirated abroad? There is probably very little that you can do, as even the largest publishing companies have made minimal progress in preventing this practice.

ENGINEERING WORKS

Engineering works, such as proposals and blueprints, are protected poorly by copyrights. Copyrights protect only the expression of ideas or concepts, not the ideas or concepts themselves. This is unfortunate, because it is likely that you are not as interested in protecting your prose as in protecting the ideas your words describe.

Nevertheless, protecting the expression is the best you can do under copyright law. You can copyright your description and drawing of a product, thereby preventing someone else from exactly copying those works. If someone sees your plans, however, and if he can duplicate the product without actually having a copy of your plans, he is free to do so. A copyright in your writings and illustrations might be sufficient, however, due to the complexity typical of most engineering plans. In these cases, a would-be infringer will be unable to build from your idea without having a copy of your plans.

This presents you with a dilemma. Registering your work with the Copyright Office makes details of the work available to the public, so you should not register anything you want kept secret. On the other hand, you need to have registered your work in order to sue an infringer.

The best thing to do in such a case probably is to refrain from registering your work, at least until you anticipate widespread distribution. Until you complete the registration process, you might want to rely on nondisclosure agreements with individuals to whom you show your works.[7] Your copyrights are reserved upon the works' creation, whether or not you register them. If you do decide to sue someone for infringement, however, you would have to register the work. Registering after the infringement takes place makes you ineligible for statutory damages and attorney's fees, but at least you can stop the infringement and collect actual damages.

Works made for a client. The law not only protects the works you create for yourself, it also covers works you create for a client. For instance, if a client asks you to create plans for a particular product, you can retain ownership if there is an agreement that the client is to return the plans to you when

---

[7]See Appendix D.

he is no longer using them for the specific purpose he discussed with you. Such a prior agreement is needed if the work-made-for-hire law is not to apply. He has no right to reuse the work or to lend, sell, or give it to anyone else. Furthermore, if your client does allow your work to be used in an unauthorized manner, you might be able to hold him responsible for the misuse.

To retain maximum control and rights regarding your work created for a client, you should place the copyright notice on each copy of each document, and get in writing all agreements concerning ownership and disclosure of engineering plans. Place a statement concerning ownership on each document, as well. Some engineers use statements like this:

> The use of these drawings and specifications shall be restricted to the original use for which they were prepared and publication thereof is expressly limited to such use. Reuse, reproduction, or publication by any method, in whole or part, is prohibited without the written consent of the engineer. Title to the designs remains with the engineer without prejudice. Visual contact with these drawings constitutes prima facie evidence of the acceptance of these restrictions.

SOFTWARE   You will encounter special problems if you want to copyright computer programs (software). Protecting computer programs, of course, was beyond the intentions of the authors of the 1909 Copyright Act. Over the years, the courts have struggled with the problem of how software fits into copyright protection. Application of copyright law to software is in a state of flux.

Nevertheless, you can protect your software to a great degree. Much of the process is the same for software as for other literary works. You should, however, be aware of some limitations.

What you can copyright. You can copyright only your program's source code (i.e., what you actually write). You can protect your object code (i.e., the computer-compiled code), the program's function (in some cases), and possibly the name of your program, in ways that are covered elsewhere in this book.

As with all other forms of literary documents, your program must be original to be copyrighted. For instance, you cannot copyright a simple counting or timing loop that does nothing original.

The same rules concerning what not to copyright, and how to renew copyrights granted before 1978, also apply to software. Also, you must use copyright notice for all works created prior to March 1, 1989.

Registering your program. To register a program, you must send Form TX with the proper fee to the Copyright Office. If your program is published, include either a diskette that contains the object code or two copies of the first and last 25 pages of a listing of the source code, if the source code is not a trade secret. (Some experts say you are better protected if you send the entire text, not just the first and last 25 pages, of a program listing that is longer than 50 pages.) The more comments that appear in the source code listing, the easier it probably will be to prove that the program is yours. If you deposit only the program's object code, however, the resulting registration is considered a "risk of doubt" registration because the Copyright Office cannot read object code.

Some experts believe that you actually are protecting the source code by filing a listing of the object code, although this point has been litigated. The primary reason for registering the object code is that object code almost always is legible only to a computer. This prevents others from reading the copy of your program registered in the Copyright Office.

Source codes. On the other hand, if you do not consider your source code a secret (see Trade Secrets elsewhere in this book), you might wish to register the first and last 25 pages of that code, as well. The Copyright Office does not require a copy of the entire program unless it is less than 50 pages long.

Usually, however, it is best to invoke trade secret status for your source code to prevent anyone from ever seeing it. In this case, you would either not register the source code or petition the copyright office to permit the deposit of only the first and last 10 pages of source code to avoid disclosing trade secrets. If you do not want to register your source code, at least include a copyright notice on any copies of it you might have, especially if you intend to distribute them.

Registration might be unnecessarily risky, particularly if you doubt that a competitor would be able to write a program to do the same thing—even if he disassembles your object code—without seeing your source code. In that case, you might want to refrain from registering your program until you think you might need to assert your copyright, if at all.

Copyright notice. It is particularly important that you place the copyright notice on all programs created prior to March 1, 1989. As with other documents, all copies of your source code must bear proper notice. Remember the proper format: either "Copyright," "Copyr.," or the © symbol, plus the year of publication (or of registration if the work is unpublished), and the copyright owner's name. Also remember that, if the work is made-for-hire, the employer owns the copyright. Placing "All rights reserved" with your notice provides the same international protection for software as for other copyrighted material.

You must also place the copyright notice on every diskette that contains your program, and it should appear on the screen every time your program is run. Note that most computers do not have a © symbol. Do not make the mistake of using (C) (a letter C in parentheses) to replace the © copyright symbol. Using (C) alone is the same as excluding a copyright notice, and will forfeit your protection until you correct the omission.

Shrink-wrap laws. Some states have enacted so-called "shrink-wrap" laws, which stipulate that removing the plastic shrink-wrap from a software package constitutes the purchaser's agreement to the conditions of sale displayed *on* (not in) the package. The conditions usually specify that the purchaser cannot copy in any manner the contents of the package. The validity of shrink-wrap licenses is unclear.

Revisions and derivative works. You should copyright new versions of programs and programs that are based on other programs. Even if the changes are slight, copyrighting the new versions can help protect them.

Related material. You also should register your user, installation, and troubleshooting manuals, and any descriptive material concerning your program, such as advertising copy and packaging. Do not forget to place copyright notices on these items.

Infringement. Someone can infringe your software copyright in one of two ways. First, he can copy the code, perhaps with the intention of selling it under a different name. Second, he can duplicate the entire program, e.g., from one diskette to another, without your authorization. You can take action against both types of infringement.

PROFESSIONAL PUBLICATIONS, INC. ● Belmont, CA

Catching infringers of your program copyright is usually more difficult than catching someone who infringes your copyright in other types of material. Part of the difficulty is that you might not know who is doing the copying. It is your responsibility to monitor new programs that seem similar in function to yours.

If you know that someone is copying your work, you will probably have more trouble proving infringement than you would if he copied another type of document. Code copiers are especially difficult to stop, because someone judging the similarity of your work and the supposedly copied one cannot look as easily for whole sections and routines copied verbatim. Most likely, a copied version will look significantly different. You might want to insert into your programs some initials, meaningless phrases, or commands that do nothing. If those commands show up in someone else's program that looks similar or performs similarly to yours, you can prove more readily that the work was copied.

Reverse engineering. Reverse engineering of computer programs is entirely legal. You cannot stop someone from studying how your program works, or even disassembling it, and then developing his own program from what he learns.

Screen displays. You might also want to register the screen displays of your particular program. For example, you might not want anyone to copy an original design or sequence that your program creates on the screen. This might seem redundant if you have registered the entire program, but this additional precaution might increase protection.

The more unusual and complex the screen is, the more you will want to protect it. Software art and computer game screens are good examples. You can register static screens by sending Form PA, the filing fee, and photographs of the screens. You can register changing screens by sending Form VA, the filing fee, and a videotape of the screens. Forms PA and VA are for protecting only the screens, however. You still will need Form TX to protect the program. Remember that the copyright notice must appear in the program listing and on the screen.

Not all screens are registrable, however. You cannot register database screens, spreadsheets, business graph generators, or word processing screens, for example.

Reiteration. To reiterate, placing copyright notices on copies of your source code protects you against someone copying the source code. Placing copyright notices on your diskettes and on the screen protects you against someone copying the object code from one diskette to another.

SEMICONDUCTOR CHIP MASK WORKS
Protecting the masks from which semiconductor chips are made has been problematic. Fortunately, legislation has begun to deal with the difficulties.

Semiconductor Chip Act. For years, semiconductor companies and designers, lawyers, judges, and juries have debated the possibility of extending copyright protection to semiconductor chips. The Semiconductor Chip Protection Act, which was meant to reduce legal difficulties arising from mask works, became law in 1984.

What is protected. The Chip Act does not actually grant protection to the chips themselves, but to the images or patterns on the masks from which chips are made. The act protects these elements even though, in contrast with copyright law, they are purely functional, not ornamental.

When protection begins. Protection under the act begins on the date the mask work is registered in the Copyright Office if the mask work already has been exploited commercially. Protection of a mask work registered in the Copyright Office but not yet exploited commercially begins the date of first commercial exploitation anywhere in the world.

Under the Semiconductor Chip Act, the Copyright Office will register a mask only if the design is original, is not a standard in the semiconductor industry, and was first commercially exploited on or after July 1, 1983.[8] Masks first exploited between July 1, 1983 and November 9, 1984 are protected if they were registered before July 1, 1985. All chip masks first exploited before July 1, 1983, and those first exploited after July 1, 1983 and before November 9, 1984, but not registered by July 1, 1985, might be protected by state laws, but are ineligible for federal registration.

---

[8]To exploit a mask work is to distribute chips produced from it to the public for commercial purposes. Distribution includes offering, in writing, to sell or transfer such chips, provided the chip that embodies the mask work already exists.

In practice, the Copyright Office has applied a "de minimus" standard to reject mask works that appear to be simple designs. For some technologies, such as microwave chip mask works, what appears to be simple is, in fact, a complex design for particular applications. In such cases, an administrative appeal can result in a registration being granted.

Chip protection differs from protection of other types of copyrightable works in one particularly important way. You must register your mask work with the Copyright Office within two years of the mask's first commercial use in the U.S. or abroad. Protection is not automatically conferred upon creation.

How to register. To register a mask work, send a completed Form MW, a filing fee, and samples. The sample requirement for commercially exploited works is four chips (dies) as first exploited and one set of reproductions of each mask work layer. The reproductions can be plastic color overlays, composite plots, or photographs of the layers, magnified 20 to 30 times their actual size.

For unexploited mask works, you must submit overlays or composite plots of each layer. You do not need to send the chips themselves.

In cases where such full disclosure is undesirable, you have another option. If filing overlays, plots, or photographs of your mask work's layers would reveal a trade secret, you may withhold reproductions of one or two layers of a mask work that consists of five or more layers. If the work is exploited, send four chips plus a printout reproduced in microfilm of the work's design data pertaining to each withheld layer. Block out or strip the sensitive material from the deposit. If the work is unexploited, send microfilm reproductions with the sensitive material blocked out or stripped, and a photograph of the work's top layer and any other layer visible from a single exposure.

The Copyright Office might grant exceptions to these trade secret requirements for masks. If you feel additional protection is needed, you can petition the Chief of the Examining Division.

Try to register. You should attempt to register any mask that is worth more than the filing fee, even if you believe the Copyright Office will reject it as being too standard or unoriginal. You will need to certify that you at least attempted to register your mask work if you intend to sue someone for infringement.

Copyright notice. Also, unlike other forms of copyrightable material, chip masks do not need to display a copyright notice to be protected. To help avoid unauthorized copying, however, you should affix a notice on the mask or on chips made from the mask. The Copyright Office requires the copyright notice to consist of the owner's name plus the words, "mask work," the symbol *M* (the letter M preceded and followed by an asterisk), or a Ⓜ symbol (a TM in a circle). You do not need to include the year. A mask work notice might look like this:

Ⓜ John Doe

Term of protection. Mask work protection is valid for 10 years, and is not renewable. This term is shorter for mask works than for other copyrightable works.

Foreign protection. A valuable mask work in the U.S. is likely to be just as valuable in another country. The Chip Act recognizes the potential international market for a good mask. The act established a three-year transition period, ending November 1987, during which foreign individuals could register masks first commercially used outside the U.S., but only if the Secretary of Commerce determined that the country of which the individual is a citizen is taking proper steps toward similar chip protection laws, or toward signing a chip treaty with the U.S.

Infringement. You can sue for infringement of a mask only if you are the owner of the work (i.e., its creator or the creator's agent), or if you have been granted all rights to it through transfer or license. You cannot sue someone who infringed more than three years before the suit is brought.

Also, you cannot sue an innocent purchaser of a semiconductor chip product that was copied from your mask. An *innocent purchaser* is someone who imported or distributed the goods without knowing the mask was copied and did so before being notified that the goods infringe a protected work. Reasonable grounds to believe a mask is protected constitutes notice of protection. An innocent purchaser must pay a royalty, of an amount to be decided in court, on infringing chips he bought prior to receiving notice of protection but imported or distributed after receiving notice. Individuals who buy chips from an innocent purchaser are not liable.

Damages imposed on mask work infringers are similar to those imposed on infringers of other protected works. A court might award the work's owner actual damages and the infringer's profits, or, if the owner requests, the court might grant statutory damages of up to $250,000. The court also will decide whether or not to restrain the infringer from distributing more copied chips, or to order infringing chips to be seized or destroyed.

ROM protection. Whether or not the Chip Act covers read-only memory (ROM) chips remains to be clarified by the government and the courts. Recent cases indicate that ROMs are protected if they meet the same criteria by which other works are judged: they must be original and nonstandard, and must meet the same manufacturing requirements. Some court cases also have upheld copyright protection for software stored in ROM.

Hardware boards. It also remains unclear whether or not hardware boards are patentable. You clearly can protect the artwork for them, however, by registering copyrights in the drawings.

PATENTS

Patents protect new and useful inventions. They are more complicated, more expensive, and more difficult to obtain than copyrights. Patents also differ from copyrights in that, while ideas are not patentable as such, a well-drafted patent claim will protect the concept of an invention. The U.S. Patent and Trademark Office, located in Arlington, VA, reviews all applications for patents.

TYPES OF PATENTS

The Patent and Trademark Office grants three types of patents:

- Plant patents protect newly developed plants that were produced asexually, such as by grafting or by rooting cuttings. Plant patents are not covered in this book.
- Design patents cover nonobvious, original appearances given to new or existing products.
- Utility patents, the most common type of patents, protect inventions.

UTILITY PATENTS

According to patent law, an *invention* is a novel and useful idea that has been *reduced to practice*. Having been reduced to practice means that the idea works, or has been described in detail in a patent application.

What can be patented. Not all inventions are patentable, however. To be patentable, an invention must be a useful process, machine, manufacturing method, composition of matter, or a new and useful improvement thereof. The invention must be original. It also must be new, which means it was never known or used by anyone else in the U.S., and was never patented or described in writing anywhere. Also, you must not have received an inventor's certificate or patent in another country for the invention more than a year before you file in the U.S.

PROFESSIONAL PUBLICATIONS, INC. ● Belmont, CA

Another hurdle is the nebulous *nonobviousness* requirement. This stipulates that a patent cannot be obtained for an invention or improvement of prior art if the invention or improvement would have been obvious to someone with ordinary skill in the invention's field.

Attorneys. Clearly, the requirements alone for obtaining a patent merit the advice of professional legal counsel. You should hire a patent attorney as early as possible. Patent attorneys have degrees in both law and engineering.

Conducting a patent search. Your attorney will assist you in the patenting process. First, a patent search will be conducted to ensure that the invention has not been patented before. The results of this search will help you decide whether or not your invention can or should be patented. Although the results of the search might disappoint you, they also might save you time and money later on. Furthermore, if the search uncovers "prior art" similar to your invention, you might be able to redesign your work to be substantially different.

Your attorney should know as much about your invention as possible before he begins your patent application. This will help ensure that your patent, if granted, gives you the broadest possible protection without making the validity of your patent questionable due to claims that are too broad. Your patent might be invalid if your invention does not live up to all of the assertions in your patent application, and such assertions can be used against you if you are sued for personal injury caused by your invention.

The application. Your patent attorney will prepare your application. A well-prepared application describes your invention in sufficient detail for someone skilled in the appropriate field to make and use it. Nevertheless, the language used on the application should be understandable to someone without a technical background. Few judges have engineering degrees, so avoid technical language wherever possible.

Your application should present the most closely related *prior art* (previous contributions to the technology that your invention advances) of which you are aware. Intentionally omitting relevant information might result in the denial or invalidation of a patent.

Your patent application also must include a description of what you believe to be the best mode for producing your invention. The language, here as elsewhere, must be straightforward and easily understood.

The patent attorney might want to use the *means plus function* format to describe your invention. This format expresses a means or step for performing a specified function without having to describe the structure, material, or acts required to perform that function. The means plus function format is helpful if describing the means by which your invention performs a function is easier than describing your invention's structure.

Another application format option is the *product by process* claim, in which you describe the process or method for producing your invention. This approach is sometimes problematic. In fact, until 1974, the Patent Office allowed product by process applications only when the invention was otherwise indescribable. The Patent Office's official policy has subsequently become somewhat more lenient.

The claims section of your application requires particular care, because claims constitute the core of what you seek to protect. They are also the basis for court decisions regarding your patented invention.

Each claim is one sentence, usually consisting of a list of clauses. The claims section typically begins "I claim," "We claim," or "What is claimed is." The preamble, which is a summary of the type of invention you are seeking to patent, usually a brief phrase, comes next. In the transition, usually just the word "comprising," follows. Last is the body of the claim, listing the specific "elements"—the features of your invention, including those that are unique, that you want covered by the patent.

The Patent and Trademark Office also accepts claims in what is known as the *Jepson-type format*. This format contains a description of the invention's conventional or known elements in the claim's preamble, a transition phrase such as "wherein the improvement comprises," and the new or improved elements of the invention. Your patent attorney will know if the Jepson-type format is your best approach.

A declaration, or oath, completes the patent application. Your signature on this document means that you reviewed and understood the patent application, that you believe you are the original inventor of what you seek to patent, and that you will give the Patent and Trademark Office any additional material it requests.

Fees. You also must enclose a fee with the patent application. The Patent and Trademark Office will levy additional fees based on the number and type of claims on your application. If your application is successful, the Patent Office will also charge you to issue the patent. You also must pay maintenance fees to keep an issued patent in force. These fees are listed in Appendix B.

Small entity status. You might be able to reduce all fees by 50 percent i you qualify for *small entity status*. To do this you must file a statemen before or with the first fee you pay as a small entity, claiming that you are one of the following:

- a sole inventor who has not transferred the patent rights to anyone who is not a small entity
- one of two or more joint investors, none of whom has transferred hi rights
- a nonprofit organization
- a business with 500 or fewer full-time, part-time, and temporar employees during the business's fiscal year

Falsifying a small entity statement constitutes fraud and can result in the patent application's rejection. An error not resulting from gross negligenc can be corrected and excused by making up the difference in fees. You must inform the Patent and Trademark Office if at any time you no longer qualif as a small entity. From then on, you will have to pay the entire fee, unless you again qualify as a small entity.

Effective filing date for applications sent via Express Mail. The Pater and Trademark Office will accept your application's postmark as your filin date if you send the application via Express Mail. The document you sen must bear a certificate of mailing signed by the person who mailed the pacl age, and include the Express Mail label number, the date of mailing, and th title and address of the Commissioner of Patents and Trademarks. An exan ple of a certificate of mailing by Express Mail can be found in Appendix G.

Using "Patent Pending." The period between the date the Patent ar Trademark Office receives your application and the date the patent is grante or the application abandoned is the *prosecution period*. During this time, th application is said to be pending. While your application is pending, you ca place the phrase "Patent Pending" or "Patent Applied For" on each copy of your invention, on products that embody your invention, and on literatu and other materials relating to the invention. This notation signifies only th you have applied for a patent, not that the Patent and Trademark Office h begun to review the application or has granted a patent.

A "Patent Pending" notice gives you no legal protection. The notice might discourage competitors from copying your potentially patented invention, but it does not legally forbid them. Furthermore, a competitor may independently develop and market, without liability, a similar or identical invention during the period your patent is pending.

Information disclosure (or, prior art) statement. Every individual associated with the filing of a patent application, including the inventor and the inventor's patent attorney, has a duty to disclose to the Patent Office information known to them that is material to the patentability of any claim in the application. Information is material if it is not cumulative to other information already of record and when it either:

- establishes, by itself or in combination with other information, a prima facie case of unpatentability; or
- refutes a position the applicant has taken in opposing a position taken by the Patent Office, or in asserting an argument of patentability.

A prima facie case of unpatentability occurs when every element of the claim in issue is found in a single prior art reference or in a combination of prior art references that include a suggestion to combine elements to produce the claimed invention. Failure to disclose known, material information in violation of the duty of disclosure can make your patent unenforceable against infringers.

The duty of disclosure is met by filing an information disclosure statement. An information disclosure statement includes a list of all patents, publications and other information submitted for consideration, a legible copy of the same, and a concise explanation of the relevance of each item submitted that is not in the English language. If a written English translation of a non-English language document, or a portion thereof, is in the possession or control or is readily available to a person involved with the prosecution of the application, it must accompany the statement.

The information disclosure statement must be filed within three months of the U.S. filing date of the application, or before the mailing date of a first office action, whichever occurs later. If an information disclosure statement is not filed before the later of these two dates, it will not be considered by the examiner without payment of a $200 fee and the filing of a petition explaining why the statement was filed late. If you find you have not met the deadline for filing an information disclosure statement, you should consult with your attorney since it may be safer to file a continuation application than to file a petition for a late information disclosure statement.

Application review. The Patent and Trademark Office will review your application for completeness shortly after receiving it. If the application is satisfactory, the office will assign it a filing date and a serial number, and will send it to the examination group assigned to your type of invention. The examination group, in turn, will send your application to one of its examiners. These first steps can take several months.

The examiner will review your application and, by means of an *Office Action*, will inform you that your application has been accepted and has proceeded to the next step, or that you need to make specified changes on the application to make it acceptable and what further information you should send. The examiner might issue several Office Actions, responding each time to your latest response.

Do not be discouraged if an examiner rejects many or even all of your original claims. He might simply want you to defend more extensively the claims you have made.

You are entitled to at least one further examination after receiving an Office Action. You can make none, some, or all of the examiner's suggested changes, additions, or deletions before requesting a further examination. Many applications generate several Office Actions and applicant responses before the Patent and Trademark Office approves further processing or issues a final rejection.

You normally need to respond to an Office Action within three months from the date the Patent and Trademark Office mailed it. The Patent and Trademark Office will grant an extension if you request it and include the required fee, but you cannot wait longer than six months to respond. If you do not file a response within six months (with the requisite fee for the extension period if your response is filed after three months), or if you fail to meet any other designated deadline, your application is abandoned, and you will not receive a patent.

Interviews. An examiner must grant an interview anytime prior to a final office action. After a final office action, an examiner need not, but may, grant an interview. The interview may be with the inventor, the attorney, or both. An interview is particularly helpful if you do not understand the examiner's Office Actions, or wish to discuss possible amendments to the claims to overcome any prior art cited by the examiner. Interviews can be by telephone or in person at the U.S. Patent Office. The most effective interviews are in-person interviews, because they allow more dialogue between the examiner and the applicant or his representatives. However, this can be expensive if you live outside of the Arlington, VA/Washington, D.C. area.

Rejection. If the examiner concludes that you and he have insurmountable disagreements concerning one or more of your claims, he might issue a final rejection. You can cancel the disputed claims, change them to comply, file a continuation application to renew the entire process, or appeal the rejection to the Board of Appeals. If you are unsatisfied with the Board of Appeals' decision, you can appeal to the U.S. District Court in Washington, D.C., or to the U.S. Court of Appeals for the Federal Circuit.

Allowance. The correspondence between you and the examiner, if all goes well, will result in a Notice of Allowance, telling you that he considered the application adequate to proceed to the next prosecution step. If you receive a Notice of Allowance, examine it carefully with your attorney. Check for a "reason for allowance" that your examiner might have listed. If a stated reason seems overly simple or inaccurate, notify the Patent Office; otherwise, you might encounter difficulties if your patent is later challenged.

Issuance. You have three months from the date the Patent Office mailed your Notice of Allowance to pay the issuance fee. Sometime thereafter, you should receive your Notice of Issuance, telling you your patent number and when the patent will be issued.

When you get your patent, you and your attorney should check it for typographical errors. To correct significant errors, file a petition for a certificate of correction. If the errors are the fault of the Patent and Trademark Office, there will be no fee. If the errors are your fault or your attorney's, you must enclose a fee.

Errors and changes. You can apply for a patent reissue if you find an error in your patent, as long as the mistake was not intended to deceive anyone. You must surrender your original patent before you can get a reissued patent. Your reissued patent must not include anything new other than your corrections.

You also can try to change your patent in other ways. You can send the Patent and Trademark Office a statutory disclaimer, which retracts one or more of your patent claims. This is particularly important if you anticipate litigation concerning your patent and you believe your claims are too broad or otherwise invalid.

You also can narrow the scope of your patent claims by applying for a narrowing reissue. You may do this any time during the patent's term. This is usually more difficult than filing a statutory disclaimer, however. Your attorney will help you choose the best method for narrowing your claims.

On the other hand, you might wish to broaden your patent claims. You can do this by applying for a broadening reissue within two years of the issuance date. You cannot, however, broaden your claims by filing for a corrective reissue.

Term of protection. A utility patent is valid for 17 years, beginning on the date the Patent and Trademark Office issued it. You cannot renew a patent.

Patent marks. You should notify people seeing or using your invention that it is protected. The best way is to place the word "Patent," or the abbreviation "Pat.," and the number of your patent on each copy of your invention and also on the patented part of any product that embodies your invention. This notice is not mandatory, but it is advisable. It discourages would-be infringers, and enables you to recover damages for infringement that occur before the filing of a patent infringement lawsuit.

Do not place a patent notice on anything not yet patented. Nor should you mark anything "Patent Pending" unless you really have applied for a patent. Intentional false marking is a criminal offense. You can be fined for each offense.

Your rights. As a patent owner, you have exclusive rights in your invention. A patent does not give you permission to produce your invention, although you do have that right, as long as doing so does not infringe someone else's patent. Instead, a patent gives you the right to exclude others from producing the invention for the term of your patent. In this regard, a patent is a "negative right."

A patent indicates ownership. Accordingly, you can grant others permission to use, promote, or sell your patented invention. Typically, a license is granted to another party in exchange for a royalty or other form of compensation. If you grant an exclusive license, you cannot later license someone else to use your invention. Your compensation, therefore, usually will be higher than for nonexclusive licenses. You would be well advised to have an attorney draft your licensing contracts.

Foreign patent protection. Patent protection in foreign countries usually will cost you more than protection in the U.S. As with copyright protection, there is no "international patent" that protects your invention everywhere. In many cases, the trouble and expense of foreign protection is unjustifiable.

Some countries charge high filing fees. Some charge annual maintenance fees that increase each year. Gaining foreign protection often requires hiring a lawyer or agent in each country. If you file your foreign applications within one year of your U.S. filing date, you can get the benefit of your U.S. filing date. You *must* do this if you have begun commercial use, or have published your invention after your U.S. filing date and before your foreign filing date.

Because filing patent applications in each country can be expensive, you might be better off relying on an international patent treaty. Not all countries are parties to a treaty, but many countries are. This route usually is less expensive than country-by-country filing if protection is sought in five or so member countries.

One such treaty to which the U.S. belongs is the Patent Cooperation Treaty (PCT), whereby you can apply for protection in the member countries within one year of filing in the U.S.[9] Discuss this option with your attorney if you seek protection in several foreign countries.

The European Patent Convention (EPC) can give you protection in most Western European countries.[10] To obtain EPC protection, you can submit an application either through the U.S. Patent and Trademark Office (by listing the EPC as a selected country), or through an attorney or agent in one of the EPC countries. Your application will be examined first by an EPC office in The Hague, Netherlands. The European Patent Office (EPO) in Munich, West Germany, continues the prosecution. If your application succeeds, the EPO will send copies to each designated member country. Each country then

---

[9]Major PCT members include Australia, Austria, Belgium, Denmark, Finland, France, Germany, Hungary, Japan, Netherlands, Norway, Sweden, U.S.S.R., Switzerland, U.K., and the U.S. You also can designate the European Patent Convention (EPC) in a PCT application.

[10]EPC members include Austria, Belgium, France, Germany, Italy, Liechtenstein, Luxembourg, Netherlands, Sweden, Switzerland, and the U.K.

issues you its own patent, which will be valid for 20 years from your EPC filing date.

If someone infringes your patent. Patent litigation is almost always more complicated than litigation concerning other forms of intellectual property. Patent litigation might include suing someone for infringement, or being sued by someone who wants to invalidate your patent. It is usually better to settle out of court, unless the potential market for the disputed item is very large. Patent-related suits typically cost more than $100,000 to take to trial.

You cannot sue someone for patent infringement until the Patent and Trademark Office has issued the patent. Thereafter, you can sue or seek other means to recover damages, or both.

For instance, you can sue someone who is producing or marketing your patented invention without your permission. You would sue him for *direct infringement* of your patent.

You can sue someone who encourages or helps another person infringe your patent. You would sue him for *inducement of infringement.*

Contributory infringers constitute another category of individuals you can sue. A contributory infringer is someone who sells items that can only be used to infringe your patent, sold knowingly in violation of your patent.

If you are accused of infringement. If you find your self accused of patent infringement, you and your attorney will have to choose a defense. One common defense is to attempt to prove that you did not infringe a patent. To prove this, you might demonstrate that your product does not include some or all of the elements in the patent claims.

You also can defend yourself by showing that the plaintiff's patent is invalid. You must present clear and convincing evidence that the invention is not novel, is obvious, or is insufficiently disclosed in the patent's file. This can be done, for example, by using publications that were published more than a year before the filing date of the patent and that show the invention or an obvious variation, or by showing the patented invention itself was sold or offered for sale more than a year before the filing date of the patent. Establishing invalidity is often difficult. The court will assume that the patent is valid because the Patent and Trademark Office issued it, and you must overcome this assumption.

Another possible defense is to establish that the patent holder was dishonest in his dealings with the Patent and Trademark Office. This entails proving intentional misrepresentation. If you prove this, the court might rule that the patent is unenforceable, and that you are not liable to the plaintiff. The court also might impose punishment on the plaintiff.

You also can seek to prove that the patent owner misused his patent; e.g., by violating antitrust laws. The court might excuse you from damages the plaintiff incurred while he was misusing his patent. You cannot use this defense if the patent owner was using the patent in a way that would constitute infringement if anyone else used it, if he permitted someone else to use the patent in that way, or if he tried to enforce his patent against infringement.

If a patent owner accuses you of infringing a patent, and he threatens to sue you but has not yet filed against you, you can initiate a lawsuit against him to declare the patent invalid. Making the first move gives you the advantage, because you, the plaintiff, have more control over where the case will be heard. Being the plaintiff also gives you the advantage if you agree to settle out of court.

Computer software. Software usually is best protected by copyrights. In some instances, however, you might be able to patent a computer program as part of an invention or process. Patents on software differ from copyrights on software in that patents might protect the concept of the software (e.g., the electronic spreadsheet when that concept was new).

The key to successfully patenting software is to describe on the application the integration of the software with generic hardware. The integration can be treated as an invention if it meets the usual patentability criteria; e.g., novelty and nonobviousness. Patent protection for software is a developing area of the law and you should consult an expert who is familiar with recent developments if you have a new and potentially valuable program. A substantial amount of published information concerning patents for software is obsolete and inaccurate.

DESIGN PATENTS Design patents protect an original appearance given to an object. These patents cover only novel and nonobvious appearances. Design patents, unlike utility patents, are issued only to ornamental, nonfunctional aspects of a manufactured item. Rather than protecting an item, a design patent protects only an item's *appearance*. Design patents generally are cheaper and faster to obtain than utility patents.

The application. A design patent application requires particularly detailed drawings. You must include several views of the design, so that the appearance of the design cannot be mistaken.

On your application, the specifications of your design need to include explanations only of the drawings. The claims section should have only one claim, which indicates the nature or type of manufactured item on which the design is to appear.

In most other respects, applying for a design patent is similar to applying for a utility patent. You might require the services of an attorney. Everything submitted must be an original document containing a sworn statement that the contents are accurate and true.

Term of protection. A design patent granted after 1982 is valid for 14 years. A design patent issued before the law changed in 1982 was valid for $3^1/_2$, 7, or 14 years. The patent owner chose his term before receiving the patent.

Infringement. Infringement of a design patent is handled similarly to infringement of a utility patent. You will need an attorney to handle your case.

TRADE SECRETS

Protection of trade secrets is very different from other kinds of intellectual property protection. This is principally because trade secret law usually is not statutory. No federal legislature has written trade secret laws (although some states have enacted related laws). Common law governing this area has evolved case by case. Furthermore, common law regarding trade secrets varies among the states. Despite these characteristics, trade secret law can be quite protective if the proper precautionary steps are taken.

WHAT IS A TRADE SECRET? A *trade secret* is secret or confidential information that gives your business an advantage over competitors who do not have the same information. Trade secrets might include a chemical formula, a manufacturing process, a technique, a design, computer software, an advertising strategy, a customer list, or a company budget. Because trade secret law is not governed by statute, the range of protectable information is virtually unlimited.

There are two reasons you should be aware of trade secret law. If you own a business, you probably want to protect your company secrets. Conversely, if you are employed by a company, but are planning to start your own business in competition with your current employer, you will not want your employer to sue you for stealing his trade secrets.

HOW TO PROTECT YOUR TRADE SECRETS In most cases, you should be able to design your own trade secret protection system. You probably will not need a lawyer to help you, unless you plan to use special legal contracts and agreements.

Identifying your trade secrets. The first step in protecting your trade secrets is to identify everything you consider secret. For example, you might consider the following items to be valuable trade secrets.

- employee salaries
- customer lists
- sources and suppliers
- the process for manufacturing your product
- computer program source codes
- advertising methods and plans
- plans for future products
- in-house procedure or policy manuals
- manufacturing costs
- sales and profit figures

In short, you should identify everything you do not want your competitors to know. Trade secrets cannot, however, include general business practices, such as how often you update ledgers or how your employees answer the telephone. Trade secrets, by definition, do not include anything about your company, its products, or its practices that is publicly known.

Controlling access. Restrict access to sensitive trade secrets as much as possible, and keep records of who has access to which secrets. This practice will help you limit and trace leaks. More importantly, it will show that you considered the information to be a trade secret. Also, to the extent that you can keep sensitive information away from photocopying machines and other means of copying or disseminating material.

Nondisclosure agreements. You should consider requiring new employee to sign a nondisclosure agreement. This is a document stating that the employee agrees to keep confidential, during and following his employment information about the company that, if revealed outside the company, will be detrimental. Keep the terms broad enough to cover potential changes in what you consider a trade secret, but not so broad as to render the document unclear or unenforceable.

Often, the principal value of a nondisclosure agreement is as a deterrent because a court will not always consider such an agreement fully binding on an employee. If a nondisclosure agreement becomes relevant in a lawsuit involving trade secrets, the court will judge the extent of the document enforceability according to certain criteria; e.g., whether or not the information was really secret, whether or not the source of the information was marked as confidential, and so forth.

An explicit nondisclosure agreement might not be necessary. A court might recognize a confidentiality pledge implicit in the nature of an employee work. This depends on how confidential the information handled by the employee was, how valuable to the company the information was, how closely guarded the information was, and other factors.

Keeping records. Be ready to document dollar amounts, in case the value of certain information is debated. Keep logs that detail research and development expenditures, and maintain ledgers that demonstrate revenues earned expressly from your trade secrets. Good records can help enormously in court.

Noncompetition agreements. Noncompetition agreements are also advisable.[11] An employee signing one agrees not to enter business in direct competition with your company. You must be careful with these agreements, however, and you should consult an attorney before drafting and implementing them. They must not unreasonably restrict an employee from earning a living if he leaves your company. In some states, particularly Michigan and California, noncompetition agreements might be entirely unenforceable. Statutes do not grant validity to such agreements in those states except in some very limited circumstances.

A departing employee. An employee who leaves your company to work for a competitor will probably know some of your trade secrets. In most cases, you cannot stop him from joining a competitor, but you can minimize the risk of the employee accidentally or intentionally revealing those secrets to his new employer. You might, for example, tell your departing employee, in writing and in an exit interview, what you consider a trade secret and that, even though he is leaving your employ, he is still obligated to maintain confidentiality. You cannot, however, prevent him from disclosing some of your company's general business practices or other general information.

Naturally, it is preferable to avoid litigation. Doing your best to prevent trade secret disclosure is far better than pursuing through the courts someone who has already revealed your valuable secrets.

HOW TO AVOID STEALING TRADE SECRETS By the same token, you as an employer can take steps to avoid unethical or illegal procurement of a competitor's trade secrets. Proper action now might keep you out of court and will protect your professional reputation.

---

[11]A typical noncompetition agreement appears in Appendix F.

Hiring away from a competitor. If you hire someone who has worked for a competitor, be sure the new employee understands that he is not to reveal his former company's trade secrets. You also might send the former employer a polite letter that states you have prohibited the new employee from giving you confidential information about that company. Such a letter will indicate that you are conscientious and ethical, and might prevent frivolous suits in the future.

Accidental access to trade secrets. If, despite your precautions, you accidentally receive a competitor's trade secret, keep track of where and how you obtained it. If the information becomes well known, it will lose its trade secret status and its legal protection.

COMPETING WITH A FORMER EMPLOYER You must be particularly careful if you leave your employer and establish your own business in competition with him. (This is especially true if you have signed a noncompetition agreement.) The former employer is bound to feel vulnerable toward an ex-employee who knows a number of trade secrets. This feeling might lead to legal action, merited or not.

Hiring former coworkers. The more employees you hire away from your former employer, the more worried he is likely to be. Taking coworkers with you when you start your own business requires careful maneuvering. Courts have levied sizeable damages against former employees who have recruited unethically. It is advisable to consult an attorney before you ask coworkers to quit with you to join your new company. Usually, you will be safer if you refrain from recruiting until your resignation is effective. In fact, you are safest if you refrain from even discussing your plans to form a competing company until you have left your employer.

Customer lists. Avoid taking or using customer lists that belong to your former employer, even if you compiled the lists yourself. They belong to him and he might sue you if you use them. The more carefully your former employer guarded his customer lists, the more legally liable you are held for using them. Customer lists are often considered one of the most valuable kinds of trade secrets.

Corporate opportunity laws. Some states require you to present potential money-making ideas to your employer before you quit to form your own company with the idea. Consult a lawyer to see if your idea falls under *corporate opportunity laws*, if your state has them.

SUING TRADE SECRET "THIEVES" Lawsuits associated with trade secrets are costly for both the plaintiff and defendant in time, emotional energy, and money. As with all kinds of intellectual property, both sides usually win something when they settle out of court, and both lose to varying degrees when they take their differences to a judge. This is especially true in trade secret cases, because of the tremendous amount of money required for court resolution.

It is, unfortunately, sometimes impossible to settle out of court. Although you probably should hire a lawyer if you intend to settle out of court, you will certainly need one to represent you if you go to court, either as plaintiff or defendant.

Whom you can sue. You may take legal action against the person or persons who had original access to your trade secrets, and against the individuals and companies who obtain the secrets from the "thieves." Nevertheless, you probably never will recover everything you have lost, even if you win a lawsuit.

Temporary restraining order. If a judge will not immediately issue an injunction, he might issue a *temporary restraining order*, which will put the case on hold until an injunction hearing takes place. Temporary restraining orders are less restrictive than injunctions, however, and usually remain valid for a shorter period (20 days).

Preliminary injunction. You probably will want to obtain a *preliminary injunction*. This is a court order forbidding the defendant from using what you claim to be your trade secret until a full trial begins. A judge might decide to issue an injunction immediately, or he might decide to hold an injunction hearing, during which both sides present testimony to prove whether or not an injunction is warranted.

It might take you about 30 days to obtain a preliminary injunction, and it might last for a year or more. If an injunction is issued, and the defendant violates it, he could be cited for contempt of court. An injunction could greatly hinder the defendant's business, but a failure to obtain an injunction could render impotent your lawsuit. For this reason, both parties must be well prepared for the injunction hearing.

Discovery. Prior to trial, both sides will engage in a period of *discovery*, during which each side collects from the other documents that could be relevant to the case. The documents might include depositions of employees in both companies and of third parties, such as vendors and customers. This takes a great deal of time and adds considerably to the growing expense of the lawsuit.

Expert witnesses. You might need to hire experts from outside your company to testify on your behalf. For instance, an economist who specializes in your field might be able to estimate your losses resulting from the alleged trade secret theft. An independent source usually is perceived by judges and juries as more legitimate; however, an expert witness' testimony will cost you money.

The trial date. The preliminary preparation for trial will almost certainly take several months. It might take more than a year. When a trial date finally is set, your attorney will need to devote a larger proportion of his time to your case, because he will be working with a deadline. Your attorney probably charges you by the hour, so this period and the trial itself will result in your greatest expenses.[12] Nothing—other than pride, perhaps—prevents you from settling with the defendant at this juncture. Many trade secret cases end in an out-of-court settlement, saving both sides the effort, legal fees, and invaluble time consumed by a trial.

IF YOU ARE SUED

If you are a defendant in a lawsuit over trade secrets, you should consider, with your counsel, several strategies and tactics. The best defenses require action *before* a lawsuit ensues.

Keeping records. Accurate, detailed records that document how you developed your own customer lists and your own products, and how you obtained

---

[12]You might instead hire your lawyer on a contingency basis, whereby he is paid a predetermined amount or percentage of damages only if you win the case. This fee basis, however, is rare in trade secret cases. More common is the value-determined basis, which entails set fees for the entire case, regardless of the outcome or the number of hours it takes.

your employees, will prove invaluable if you are sued for stealing trade secrets or for unfairly recruiting employees from another company. During the discovery stage of trade secret proceedings, your opponent has access to every interview, conversation, letter, and document to which you were a party, except communications with your lawyer and, sometimes, with your spouse. It pays to keep copies of the polite letters you have written to your new employee's former boss, and to emphasize to third parties that you bear no malice toward your former employer. Such evidence, when produced in court, might help convince a judge that you are not the "thief" the plaintiff claims you are.

Counter-complaints. Your attorney might advise you to proceed aggressively. If the plaintiff's case is weak, one tactic is to file a counter-complaint against the plaintiff, claiming he is guilty of holding invalid patents or violating antitrust laws, for example. This counterattack might help persuade the plaintiff to settle with you out of court.

TRADEMARKS

A *trademark* is a word, name, or symbol that you use to distinguish your products or services from those of your competitors. It usually is a brand name or logo that appears on your products. Trademarks are valuable to you, because they let your customers know which goods or services are yours, and that you assure the consistent quality of those goods or services. This section also covers other, related marks.

CATEGORIES OF MARKS

Marks fall into four categories. One is trademarks. *Service marks* are those marks you use in selling or advertising your services to distinguish them from your competitors' services. *Certifica-tion marks* are those marks you use on products or in connection with services provided by someone other than the mark's owner, which certify their quality, accuracy, origin, material, manufacturing method, or other characteristics. *Collective marks* are those marks you use to indicate that you are a member of a cooperative, association, or other collective organization. You can register as *collective membership marks* those marks that indicate your membership in a union, association, or other organization.

CHOOSING TRADEMARKS

Select your trademarks with care. The way your chosen trademarks relate to your products determines the degree to which they are protected.

Coined marks. The greatest protection is given to a trademark that you coin, and that bears not even the slightest suggestion of the nature of your product (e.g., the name "Kodak" on cameras). A coined mark is favored in court because it is intrinsically distinctive, and therefore unlikely to be already in use on other products. Thus, it is rarely difficult to register a coined mark, and it can be used on a variety of products you might produce.

PROFESSIONAL PUBLICATIONS, INC. • Belmont, CA

Arbitrary marks. The next best choice is a mark that consists of a word already in existence, but arbitrary as applied to your product (e.g., the name "Crest" on toothpaste). You can register an arbitrary mark if its use would not confuse consumers, but you probably will have to limit its use to a particular product or narrow range of products.

Suggestive marks. A suggestive mark, which hints at the nature of the product under that mark, is entitled to less protection than a coined or arbitrary mark. An example of a suggestive mark is the name "Black Flag" on a household pesticide. You might encounter some difficulty registering a suggestive mark, depending on the degree to which it suggests the nature or attributes of your product.

Descriptive marks. Descriptive marks are even more difficult to register and protect. In fact, a descriptive mark (e.g., the name "Cat Chow" on cat food) normally cannot be registered until, after a period of heavy use, the mark becomes associated virtually exclusively with your product. It takes a significant amount of consumer identification for a descriptive mark to be considered registrable.

Generic marks. Generic names (e.g., the word "Beer") cannot be protected as trademarks. Such names do not distinguish one company's product from its competitors'.

What cannot be registered as a trademark. You cannot register a trademark that is immoral, deceptive, or scandalous; that defames an institution, belief, national symbol, or a living or deceased person; or that contains the flag or other insignia of a country, state, or municipality. Also, you cannot use the name, portrait, or signature of a living person unless you have his written permission, and you cannot use the name, portrait, or signature of a deceased U.S. president during his widow's life without her written permission.

Avoiding trademark loss. Trademarks can lose protection by becoming generic names. "Xerox," because people regularly use the term generically when referring to photocopies and photocopying, might become a generic name and might lose protection. Other examples are "Band-Aid," as applied to an adhesive bandage strip, and "Kleenex," as applied to a facial tissue.

You might avoid losing your trademark protection in this manner by always referring to your product by the trademark plus the generic type of product (e.g., "Kleenex brand facial tissues"), rather than using the trademark alone to denote the product. Some companies spend many advertising dollars reminding the public not to use their trademark as a generic term. If you fear your trademark is becoming generic, you might want to do the same.

You also can lose trademark protection by abandoning your mark. Trademark protection ordinarily lasts as long as you continually use the mark, if you renew it every 20 years. If you stop using the mark for a significant period of time, you might lose your rights in that mark. If you do not use it for a two-year period, the mark is presumed to be abandoned. An abandoned mark is available to anyone who wishes to use it, and can be registered by another party that has adopted it.

State protection. Trademarks can be protected in your state, if you do not desire federal protection or such protection is unavailable to you. A trademark attorney in your state will be able to help you. State registration alone might be significantly less protective, however.

HOW TO REGISTER YOUR MARKS You can register your trademarks with the U.S. Patent and Trademark Office. You must use the trademark with goods or services in interstate commerce in order to obtain a federal trademark registration. However, you may file an Intent-To-Use application prior to actual use if you wish to reserve a trademark. An individual, firm, partnership, corporation, or association can own and register a trademark.

You must own a mark to register it. When requesting the proper forms from the Patent and Trademark Office, specify whether you are applying as an individual, a firm, or a corporation.

Trademark search. You should have an attorney conduct a trademark search before you begin to use and register your mark. You can file a trademark registration application yourself, but you might want an attorney to handle it because registration requirements are very strict.

The application and drawing. You need to submit a written application; a drawing of the mark; for a conventional application, identical specimens or facsimiles; and a fee. No specimens are required for an Intent-To-Use application. The application is fairly straightforward. Specifications for the drawing, however, are numerous and detailed. It must exactly represent your mark, must be in pure black India ink on standard-size white paper, must contain no white correction fluid, and must have a heading that includes your name, address, the date of the mark's first use, and the goods or services listed in the application. Send the drawing flat, with adequate protection, or rolled in a mailing tube.

The specimens or facsimiles. The specimens you submit must have the trademark somewhere on the product itself or on a label, tag, container, or display associated with or attached to the product. You normally cannot use advertising materials as specimens. The specimens must be flat and no larger than 8½ x 13 inches. For service marks, company business cards, brochures, or photographs of signage bearing the mark may serve as specimens.

If your specimens are too bulky or are not flat, you may instead submit facsimiles of the trademark as it is used. Facsimiles may be photographs or other clear reproductions, no larger than 8½ x 13 inches.

The Patent and Trademark Office is more lenient in its requirements for service mark specimens or facsimiles. If you cannot submit specimens or facsimiles due to the way the mark is used, you may submit a letter of explanation.

The fee. You must include a filing fee. Your payment must be payable to the Commissioner of Patents and Trademarks.

The application review. The Patent and Trademark Office reviews trademark applications in the order in which they are received. If, after a preliminary study of your application, an examiner requests more information from you, you must respond within six months or the office will consider your application abandoned.

Rejection and appeal. If the application is rejected, the office will notify you and give you its reasons. You can appeal to the Trademark Trial and Appeal Board, if you wish. There is an appeal fee.

Publication for Opposition. If no reason is found to deny registration of your trademark, the examiner will send the application to the publications branch, where your trademark will be published for opposition in the *Trademark Official Gazette*. Anyone who might be damaged by the registration of your trademark will then have 30 days from the date of publication to oppose the registration or to file an extension of time to oppose. If no oppositions or requests for extension of time to oppose are received by the Trademark Office during the 30-day period, the application will be approved and the trademark will be registered.

The registers. A successful application will allow your mark to be listed on one of two trademark registers. Coined, arbitrary, and suggestive marks, if qualified, will be registered on the *Principal Register*. This is the best register on which to list your mark, because inclusion on this register constitutes constructive notice of your rights in that mark. Your rights in the mark are difficult to challenge because marks on the Principal Register carry the presumption of validity. After five years on the Principal Register, your registration will become incontestable. This means a challenger cannot typically seek to cancel your registration.

Marks that do not qualify for the Principal Register, but have been used commercially for at least a year and serve to distinguish your products or services from those of someone else, will be added to the Supplemental Register. Although a mark on the *Supplemental Register* does not carry the same strong presumptions as one on the Principal Register, you may ask a court to help preserve your rights in the mark if you feel the mark is being infringed. A mark on the Supplemental Register can be transferred later to the Principal Register if the mark becomes eligible.

Continued use. To keep your registration in force, you need to file with the Patent and Trademark Office, between the fifth and sixth year following the original registration's issue date, an affidavit of continued use. You might have to send proof that you are still using the mark. Such proof might include product packaging or advertising that bears both the mark and an indication of the product or service attributes your customers associate with the mark.

Renewal. Trademark registrations issued before November 16, 1989 expire 20 years after the registration issues. Registrations issued on or after November 16, 1989 expire 10 years after the registration issues. You can renew either type of registration for further 10-year periods by filing a renewal application during the six-month period prior to the expiration date. Such applications may also be filed during the three-month period after the expiration date if an additional fee is paid. Renewal applications are handled much like initial applications, and require a specimen of the mark, a renewal fee, and a statement that the mark is still in use.

TRADEMARK NOTICE

As with copyrights and patents, trademarks require that you give adequate public notice that your mark is protected in order to achieve maximum protection against infringers. The symbol TM, often used as a superscript, indicates that the word or design preceding it is claimed as a trademark by the owner. Once federal registration is obtained for the mark, always place with the mark the words "Registered in U.S. Patent and Trademark Office," the abbreviations "Reg. U.S. Pat. and Tm. Off.," or the symbol ® (the letter R in a circle) to denote the registered trademark. This is used instead of the symbol TM. Do not use any of these demarcations if your mark is registered only in your state.

FOREIGN TRADEMARK PROTECTION

Foreign trademark protection is possible, sometimes even before you begin to use the mark. Check with your attorney or the government of each country in which you intend to use the mark.

PROTECTING YOUR TRADEMARK

You have the right to use your trademark to distinguish your products or services from your competitors'. If a competitor uses your mark, or one similar enough when applied to goods or services to confuse a consumer, you must take steps to protect your mark and the goodwill it represents.

Infringement. You have legal recourse if you believe someone is infringing your trademark, even if the alleged infringement is unintentional. The first step, of course, is to hire an attorney.

You might be able to obtain an injunction against someone who you can prove is about to infringe your trademark. This would prevent possible infringement until a trial can determine conclusively whether or not the new mark infringes yours.

You also can ask a judge to issue a writ of attachment if you believe the defendant might move his funds abroad to prevent losing them to you in court. A writ of attachment prevents the defendant from moving his funds until the trial ends.

After an infringement occurs, you can sue for damages as well as for an injunction. A judge might award you part or all of the infringer's profits or your lost profits. If the infringer's actions have been blatantly illegal, the judge might grant you punitive damages and attorney's fees, as well. He also might award you a combination of these damages.

TRADE NAMES AND FICTITIOUS NAMES

A *trade name* is simply the name by which the public knows your business. It is virtually the same as a *fictitious name*, which is a commercially used name that does not fully identify its user.

REGISTRATION   Both trade names and fictitious names can be registered with most state governments. If your trade name is also a fictitious name, you probably can protect it by registering it as one or the other. Trade name registration is usually stronger. Contact the appropriate government office in your state.

PROFESSIONAL PUBLICATIONS, INC. ● Belmont, CA

BIBLIOGRAPHY

"At last, a law to catch the chip pirates." *Businessweek*, October 22, 1984, p. 39.

Becker, Stephen A. "Taking care of your trademark." *PC Magazine*, February 21, 1984, pp. 473–474, 479–480.

Bunnin, Brad and Peter Beren. *Author Law & Strategies*, Nolo Press, 1983.

Burge, David A. *Patent and Trademark Tactics and Practice*, 2nd Ed. John Wiley & Sons, Inc., 1984.

Burke, Alexander J., Jr. "Book piracy: A worldwide threat to authors and publishers." *Imprint*, Spring 1985, pp. 4–5.

Kaliski, Edward J. "Protecting your intellectual property." *Mechanical Engineering*, January 1978, pp. 27–31.

Miller, Peggy A., Esq. "How the new Semiconductor Chip Protection Act affects your company." *Computer Advertising News*, January 1985, pp. 12, 20.

"No chips off the old block." *Newsweek*, October 22, 1984, p. 80.

Ostrower, Donald A., Esq., P.E., and James Forster. "Protecting against unauthorized reuse of plans." *Consulting Engineer*, August 1980, pp. 16, 19–20.

Pooley, James. *Trade Secrets: How to Protect Your Ideas and Assets*, Osborne/McGraw-Hill, 1982.

Posch, Robert J., Jr. "Register your trademark and protect the image you're selling." *Direct Marketing*, September 1983, pp. 116–120.

Ranney, Elizabeth. "Software publishers seek patents." *InfoWorld*, September 1985, pp. 5–6.

Remer, Daniel. *Legal Care for Your Software*, Nolo Press, 1982, 1984.

Ross, Andrew, Esq. "Trade secrets: What are they and when are they protected?" *Engineering Perspective*, February 1983, p. 7.

Schwartz, Harry K., Esq., and Charles J. Hardy, Esq. "What the new copyright law means to engineers." *Professional Engineer*, June 1977, pp. 32–33.

APPENDIX A

IMPORTANT ADDRESSES

Commissioner of Patents and Trademarks
    Patent and Trademark Office
    Washington, DC 20231
    (703) 557-3881

    This office supplies application forms for registering trademarks, and information regarding trademarks and patents.

Copyright Office
    Information and Publication Section, LM-455
    Library of Congress
    Washington, DC 20559
    (202) 707-9100 if you know which forms you need
    (202) 479-0700 if you do not know which forms you need
    (Public Information)

    This office supplies information circulars and application forms for copyright registration. Specify the quantity and type of forms you need. They are free of charge. The office takes calls from 8:30 a.m. to 5 p.m., Eastern time, weekdays except holidays. You can leave a message on a recording machine any other time. You should receive the forms in about two weeks.

    You can obtain up to five copies of the basic application forms from a local branch of the Copyright Office, if one is in your area.

PROFESSIONAL PUBLICATIONS, INC. ● Belmont, CA

APPENDIX B

FEES AS OF DECEMBER 16, 1991

Copyrights

Filing fee	$20
Renewal fee	12
Filing fee for mask works	20
Additional fee for expedited registration	200
Recording copyright assignments (one title)	20
Additional fee for 10 titles or fraction thereof	10

Patents[a]

Basic filing fee	$690
Each independent claim over three	72
Each claim of any type over 20	20
Additional fee for one or more multiple dependent claims	220
Design patent filing fee	280
Issue fee	1,130
Design patent issue fee	400
Maintenance fees	
for utility patents issued from applications filed before December 12, 1980	0
for utility patents issued from applications filed on or after December 12, 1980	
$3\frac{1}{2}$ years from issuance	900
$7\frac{1}{2}$ years from issuance	1,810
$11\frac{1}{2}$ years from issuance	2,730
for design patents	0
Recording patent assignments, per document	40

Trademarks[b]

Application fee, for registration per class	$200
Renewal fee, per class	300
Renewal fee after expiration date, per class	400

---

[a]The small entity fee usually is half the amount shown.

[b]There are no small entity rates for trademarks.

Appeal to Trademark Trial and Appeal Board, per class 100
Filing Section No. 8 affidavit, per class 100
Filing Section No. 15 affidavit, per class 100
Recording trademark assigment, agreement or
    other paper-first mark per document 40
For subsequent marks, same document 25

PROFESSIONAL PUBLICATIONS, INC. • Belmont, CA

APPENDIX C

GLOSSARY OF TERMS

Author. In regard to copyrights, the legal owner of a literary work. Not necessarily the person who wrote the work.

Certification Mark. A mark used on the products, or in connection with the services, of someone other than the mark's owner, to certify the quality, accuracy, origin, material, manufacturing method, or other characteristics of the products or services.

Collective Mark. A mark used to indicate membership in a cooperative, association, or other collective organization.

Collective Membership Mark. A mark used to indicate membership in a union, association, or other organization.

Contributory Infringement. Selling items used to infringe a patent, knowingly in violation of the patent.

Copyright. Statutory protection granted to literary works. Gives owner the exclusive right to reproduce the work.

Corporate Opportunity Laws. Laws requiring employees to present potential money-making ideas to their employers before quitting to form their own company with the idea.

Direct Infringement. Producing or marketing a patented invention without the patent owner's permission.

Discovery. A period preceding a patent, trademark, or copyright infringement, trade secret, or other trial during which each side collects from the other documents that might relate to the case.

Fair Use. Certain uses of copyrightable material that do not constitute infringement, e.g., criticism, comment, news reporting, teaching, scholarship, or research.

Fictitious Name. A commercially used name that does not fully identify the user.

Fixed and Tangible Form. In permanent, tangible form, e.g., in print or on a recording.

Inducement of Infringement. Encouraging or aiding another person to infringe a patent.

Intellectual Property. Certain creative works, e.g., original literature, computer software, trademarks, trade secrets, semiconductor chip masks, and inventions.

Invention. A novel and useful idea that has been reduced to practice.

Jepson-Type Format. A format for claims on a patent application, containing a description of a particular invention's known elements, a transition phrase, and the new elements.

Means Plus Function Format. Patent application claim format that expresses a means or step by which a particular invention performs a specified function without having to describe the structure, material, or acts required to perform the function.

Nonobviousness. Would not have been obvious to someone with ordinary skill in a particular invention's field.

Notice of Allowance. A notice sent by the Patent and Trademark Office signifying that the examiner has approved a patent application for further processing.

Office Action. An action taken by the Patent and Trademark Office that requires a response from the applicant.

Patent. Legal protection for inventions. Patents also might protect the concepts of the inventions.

Preliminary Injunction. A court order that forbids a defendant in a trade secret case from using the trade secret in question until a full trial can be held.

Principal Register. One of two federal registers of trademarks and other marks. Marks on this register carry the presumption of validity.

Prior Art. Previous contributions to the technology that a new invention advances.

Product by Process. Patent application format that describes the process or method for producing a particular invention.

Prosecution Period. Period between the date the Patent and Trademark Office receives a patent application and the date the patent is granted or the application abandoned.

Public Domain. Works that belong to the public and, therefore, are uncopyrightable.

Publication. The distribution of copies of a work to the public by sale or other transfer of ownership, or by rental, lease, or lending.

Service Mark. A mark used by a business in selling or advertising its services to distinguish them from its competitors' services.

Small Entity Status. Status as a sole inventor, joint inventors, a nonprofit organization, or a business with 500 or fewer employees, which enables the entity to reduce by 50 percent its patent fees.

Supplemental Register. One of two federal registers of trademarks and other marks. Marks on this register do not carry the presumption of validity.

Temporary Restraining Order. A court order that temporarily freezes the business of a trade secret case defendant. It is less restrictive than an injunction.

Trade Name. The name by which the public knows a particular business.

Trade Secret. Information that gives a business an advantage over competitors who do not have the information.

Trademark. A word, name, or symbol that a business uses to distinguish its products or services from those of its competitors.

Work-Made-For-Hire. A work created by an employee as part of his job. A work-made-for-hire belongs to employer, who is recognized as legal author and copyright owner.

Writ of Attachment. A court order that prevents a lawsuit defendant from moving his funds or other assets until the trial concludes.

APPENDIX D

SAMPLE NONDISCLOSURE AGREEMENT

This agreement is between _____ ("OWNER")
and _____ ("RECIPIENT").
Whereas OWNER possesses certain confidential information relating to
_____
_(a)
("INFORMATION"); and whereas RECIPIENT wishes to evaluate such
information to determine if a beneficial business relationship between the
parties relating to the use of the INFORMATION would be in the best inter-
ests of both parties; NOW THEREFORE, in consideration of OWNER's
agreement to furnish such information, RECIPIENT agrees to receive the
INFORMATION under the following terms.

1. RECIPIENT agrees to receive and maintain any INFORMATION provided pursuant to this Agreement, whether in written, oral, visual, or tangible form such as models or samples, in strict confidence. RECIPIENT agrees
to take reasonable precautions to prevent disclosure of OWNER's INFOR-
MATION to any third person.

2. RECIPIENT agrees not to use OWNER's INFORMATION for his/her/its
own benefit, or for the benefit of any person or entity, other than OWNER,
except as provided in any subsequent written agreement between OWNER
and RECIPIENT.

3. RECIPIENT agrees to return to OWNER upon request all tangible and
written INFORMATION furnished under this agreement and any copies of
the same that may have been made by RECIPIENT.

----

^(a)For example, information relating to manufacturing, engineering, production, storage
and/or sales activities of OWNER or new technologies being developed by OWNER, including but not limited to data, marketing and advertising plans, computer programs, customer,
client and vendor identities and records, and other information pertaining to the performance,
plans, strategies, and other business of the OWNER, that is proprietary, confidential, and/or
trade secret information of OWNER. (Note: Try to be as specific as possible in defining the
kind of information or technology that is being disclosed under the agreement.)

4. RECIPIENT's obligations under this agreement shall not apply to any INFORMATION that: was known to RECIPIENT before any disclosure was made by OWNER; is now or hereafter becomes known to the public through no breach of this agreement; or, becomes known to RECIPIENT, by a disclosure from a person or organization, other than OWNER, having no obligation to either OWNER or RECIPIENT to maintain the INFORMATION in confidence.

RECIPIENT:

_____
Signature

_____   _____
Printed Name/Title   Date

APPENDIX E

EMPLOYEE/INDEPENDENT CONTRACTOR
ASSIGNMENT AGREEMENT

In consideration for his or her employment by
_____ (the "COMPANY"),
_____ (the "EMPLOYEE"),
agrees as follows:

The EMPLOYEE understands that during the course of employment with the COMPANY, the EMPLOYEE may be asked to create, write, edit, review, alter, upgrade, modify, or otherwise handle or process reports, booklets, books, manuals, other documents, illustrations, tables of data, photographs, shop drawings, blueprints, computer programs, inventions or other devices, packaging and promotional materials, and similar works that have or may have value.

The EMPLOYEE hereby expressly assigns and conveys all rights, title, and interest of all types whatsoever in connection with his/her work to the COMPANY, including but not limited to, copyrights, trademarks, service marks, patent rights, publicity rights, publication rights, marketing rights, and distribution rights, and expressly including the sole rights of copyright, sales, and distribution, as well as rights regarding titling, author's names, and the size and color of the finished works. The EMPLOYEE agrees that by assigning all rights, he/she shall be compensated solely and exclusively by his/her salary as an employee, whether made on an hourly, biweekly, monthly, lump-sum, per-unit, or other basis. This assignment shall be effective regardless of whether EMPLOYEE is an employee of the COMPANY, an independent contractor, or an agent, officer, or director of the COMPANY.

The EMPLOYEE agrees and warrants that any works produced by EMPLOYEE for the COMPANY shall be original, and shall not be the subject of any claim of ownership by any third person. EMPLOYEE agrees to attach to this agreement a dislcosure of all works created before his/her employment with COMPANY in which EMPLOYEE claims ownership.[a]

EMPLOYEE:

_____   _____
          Signature   Date

_____
     Printed or Typed Name

---

[a]If the EMPLOYEE works in California, the following notice should follow the last sentence in this clause:

> California Labor Code Section 2870 provides that this assignment shall not apply to any invention that the employee develops entirely on his or her own time without using the employer's equipment, supplies, facilities, or trade secret information, unless such inventions relate, at the time of conception or reduction, to practice of the invention to the employer's business, or actual or demonstrably anticipated research or development of the employer, or the inventions result from any work performed by the employee for the employer.

APPENDIX F

SAMPLE NONCOMPETITION AGREEMENT

In consideration for his or her employment by
_____ (the "COMPANY"),
_____ (the "EMPLOYEE"),
agrees as follows:

The EMPLOYEE agrees not to compete with the COMPANY in its current or projected areas of specialization, which include but are not limited to,
_____
$^{(a)}$

and any other business that the COMPANY may enter or engage in during the term of EMPLOYEE's employment (the "COMPANY's BUSINESS"), for a period of _____
$^{(b)}$
years in the _____
$^{(c)}$
after the termination of EMPLOYEE's employment with COMPANY. Competition includes the giving of advice or counsel to others, whether with or without fee, or developing, marketing, or selling products or services that relate to the COMPANY's BUSINESS.

EMPLOYEE:

_____   _____
Signature   Date

_____
Printed or Typed Name

_____

$^{(a)}$The identification of the COMPANY's current and projected business should be detailed to increase the agreement's chance of enforceability.

$^{(b)}$The noncompetition period should be as short as possible. No more than five years is recommended. If the geographical area is very large (i.e., an entire state or all of the United States), the time period should be much less than five years, perhaps only one or two years. If the geographical area is rather limited (e.g., a city or county), a court is more likely to enforce a longer period of noncompetition like five years.

$^{(c)}$This blank is for the geographical area of noncompetition. The area should bear some relation to the business of the COMPANY. If the COMPANY does business throughout the U.S., it would be proper to use the U.S. as the geographical area of noncompetition. Keep in mind, however, that courts do not like to enforce noncompetition agreements, and will only enforce those that are reasonable as to geographical area and time.

PROFESSIONAL PUBLICATIONS, INC. • Belmont, CA